Let's Discover

THE FLOOR
OF THE
FOREST

By Ada and Frank Graham, Jr.

Photography by Les Line

GOLDEN PRESS • NEW YORK

Western Publishing Company, Inc.
Racine, Wisconsin

This book is one of a series of Audubon Primers, sponsored by the National Audubon Society. Like the other books in the series, it is designed to focus on one particular aspect of the natural world. With you as a guide, a child's natural curiosity may be nurtured, directed and expanded.

This is a real story about real people. The adventures of the children and the discoveries they make are available to everyone. Read the story to children too young to read or make it available to those who can. It may prompt you and your young companion(s) to explore the world of nature. Exploring leads to discovery.

To prepare yourself for additional questions that may arise, refer to the "Key" on pages 44-45. It provides information that goes beyond the story itself. Besides being a useful reference, it may reawaken your own curiosity about the world in which you live.

The Authors:
Ada and Frank Graham, Jr.

Fairy tales and folk lore are often set against the backdrop of a mysterious forest. For many centuries, children have been enchanted by these tales of the forest.

A great national forest still holds traces of the original enchanted forest. Here we can see the cycle of birth, growth, and decay of which we are all a part. Here we can find ferns and club mosses, survivors of the first plant communities on earth. Here we can view the great tumbled boulders and gnarled aged trees that our primitive ancestors may have worshipped.

Magic still clings to the forest. It stirs our imaginations and lures us to adventure.

Forests are part of a nation's heritage. They have been, and are today, under relentless pressures. We have harvested them for wood products, and cleared them for farmland, and bulldozed them for highways and housing developments.

Audubon Societies, with their goal of promoting the conservation of wildlife and the natural environment, as well as other groups of people, have fought and worked hard toward preserving our forest areas. In places, forests are now "forever wild" and in other places they are kept as small living museums.

Most of us, even city dwellers, probably live not far from some woodland park, an Audubon sanctuary, or a few wooded acres in the suburbs. All of these places, still hold some traces of the original enchanted forest. So, even if you are unable to visit a great national park, there are areas where you can discover the wonders of our forests.

This story is a real-life adventure. Michael and Heather, while playing hide-and-seek in a forest, hear the music from a woodland pool; touch and are touched by ferns and old tree branches; see the wonder of color and the diversity in size and shapes of emerging wild flowers, and smell the decaying roots of trees in low wet places. This story involves discovery as well as adventure.

Read this story to a young child and then share and explore a forest-like area with your young companion(s). Open yourself to the variety of life it holds. Set out to build your own treasury of experiences in discovering the floor of a forest.

Invitation to Adventure

The forest has many good hiding places for animals, and for boys and girls too.

Michael was hiding in the forest. No one could see him in his hiding place.

He looked out through the green leaves.

Heather was searching for Michael. She peeked over rocks and around the trunks of trees.

Suddenly, Michael moved. The leaves moved too, and Heather found him.

Together, Heather and Michael wandered
deeper into the forest.

The leaves of the tall trees hid the sun.
They made shadows on the floor of the
forest.

Pale green pixie cups and bright orange
mushrooms were growing under their feet.

Michael decided to hide from Heather again. He ran down a path.

"Wait for me," Heather called after him.

"Come and find me," Michael yelled.

Roots of old trees grew in tangles across the path, and held the old trees firmly in the ground. Heather tried not to trip on the thick roots, as she followed Michael.

Michael saw a very old tree. He climbed the tree and looked down at the Indian Pipes that grew in the soft ground. Their white stems were easy to see in the dark shadows. They are not green like many other plants.

Michael pushed his way into some bushes near the old tree. He was looking for a better place to hide from Heather.

He found that he wasn't the only one hiding there. An old toad and some wild flowers seemed to be hiding too. The purple hepatica were nearly covered by dead leaves and rotting tree stumps.

Near the path, Michael spotted a large tree with two trunks. The trunks were like arms raised toward the sky. Michael explored the tree. He put his face between the two big trunks and looked back along the path.

"If I stay here, I can see Heather," he thought. "But I hope she won't see me!"

Michael stayed very still. Around him in the forest, other creatures were very still and hidden too.

Insects crept under dead leaves. A fawn lay quietly in the grass, while its mother fed nearby.

Michael spotted Heather walking along the path. She stopped near another tree. Did she see him?

No, she was looking at some sap that was oozing from the bark of the tree. Heather touched the sap. Michael could see her frown as she tried to wipe the sticky sap from her fingers.

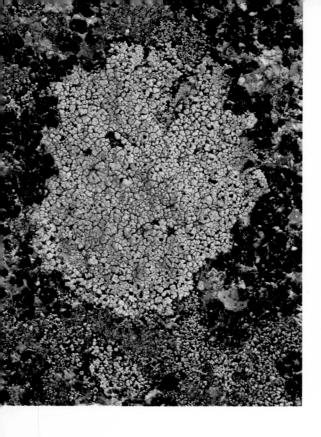

Michael wanted to keep ahead of Heather. He saw a huge rock and ran toward it. As he got down behind the rock, he ran his hand over stiff ruffled plants called *lichens,* which covered the rock.

"Come and find me," he called to Heather. "I'm not very far away."

Michael tucked himself behind the big rock. It was just right for hiding.

Suddenly, he heard a sound in the distance. Was it Heather calling to him? The sound went on and on, tinkling like music in the forest. Michael decided to see what was making the sound. As he crept along on his hands and knees, ferns, like long green hands, reached out and touched him and tickled his chin.

The tinkling sound grew louder. Michael came to a pool of water spilling over some moss-covered rocks. The water that was dripping into the pool from the rocks above it, seemed to be making the tinkling sound.

All the leaves and rocks around the pool of water smelled of wetness. Then, something moved. It startled Michael. It was a salamander hurrying to escape among the dead leaves.

Meanwhile, Heather thought she saw Michael. But when she got to the pool, he was gone. There were many trees for her to search behind. She looked around the trunk of one tree, and up into the branches of another. She looked between the two trunks of an old tree, and there she found a surprise.

At the bottom of the tree was a bird's nest, with many eggs in it. The eggs were dark and spotted. They were hard to see among the dark leaves, but Heather was delighted to have found the nest. She wondered what kind of bird had laid the eggs.

The eggs belonged to a woodcock. The mother woodcock was someplace close by. Heather knew the mother bird would come back to her eggs. So she left them undisturbed.

Meanwhile, Michael came to a low wet place. A giant tree had fallen across it like a bridge. He heard the sound of Heather's footsteps in the dry leaves behind him. He crawled along the rough tree trunk, holding onto the broken branches which stuck out from the trunk.

Could he reach the good hiding places at the other end of the fallen tree before Heather saw him?

Michael hid among the thick roots at the end of the giant tree trunk. Strange looking wild flowers, Jack-in-the-pulpits and pink Lady-slippers, were growing all around. They grow where the ground stays moist.

Heather had seen Michael at the end of the giant fallen tree. But the fallen tree was too big for Heather to climb. There were many fallen trees across the wet place. Heather found a smaller one.

She walked along the tree trunk. She had to step over its broken branches. But she never lost her balance. When Heather reached the end, she found a bright-colored tree mushroom growing from the end of the dead tree trunk.

"That's my prize for not falling," she thought.

Heather knew that Michael was somewhere nearby. She looked for him around the roots of fallen trees. She looked into the hollow of an old tree stump.

But Michael had found another hiding place. Perhaps he was looking at her right now.

Heather followed the path up a rocky hillside. She saw pretty pink blossoms among the rocks and trees.

She stooped to look at and smell the
tiny plants. Some of the pink blossoms
were turning into bright red cranberries.
The sun fell on the hillside. It warmed the
rocks and helped the berries to ripen.

Suddenly Heather turned her head.
Michael was standing near the huge
tumbled rocks high above her.

Michael had found a cave in the rocks. As he crawled into the cave, he brushed against a spider's web. It was dark and very quiet inside. The rocks felt damp, as he leaned against them.

"Heather will never find me here," he thought.

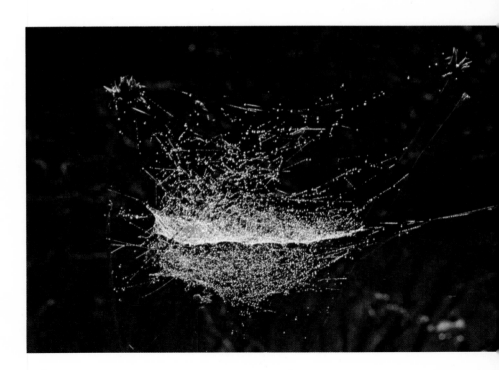

Michael heard a sound on the rocks
outside. He looked out through the narrow
opening of the cave, and saw Heather.

"Here I am," he shouted. His voice made
an echo in the cave.

"Hi!" said Heather. "You see, you can't
hide from me!"

They climbed up the hillside together.

Michael told Heather about the spider web he had seen. And Heather told Michael about the Twin-flower she had seen, and how its two pink blossoms hung together from a single stem.

When they reached the top of the hillside and looked down, they could see the giant old trees, and they knew all about the many tiny living things under and around them. Animals, wild flowers, and insects were also hiding in the shadows, on the floor of the forest.

A Key to Discovery

A forest is much more than a group of trees. When you walk through a forest, or a forest-like area, you are surrounded by an active community of plants and animals. Because there is such a variety of life in the forest, plan your trip for a certain season of the year. You will find that each season brings with it features that cannot be seen at any other time of the year.

If you bring with you some basic information and a few facts, your adventure in the forest will be enriched and the new understanding will add to your enjoyment.

First, be sure to notice how sunlight and shadows speckle the forest floor. Observe how many birds and mammals are darkly speckled too. The fawn, for example, is able to hide more easily from its enemies because its spotted coat blends into the shadowy forest. The darkly spotted eggs of a woodcock are also hard to see.

Organize your observations to get the most out of your adventure. Here are some guidelines to help you know where to begin:

ROOTS

Look at a tree's roots. Some spread out for many feet away from the tree. Others plunge into the earth beneath the tree itself. Roots anchor the tree to the forest floor. They also help to nourish the tree, drawing water and needed chemicals from the earth.

BARK

Bark is the skin of a tree. It can be rough or smooth, depending on the age or species of the tree. Run your hand over a tree's bark. Feel the differences in each kind of tree. Look for insects which may be at work in the cracks and crevices of the bark. Look closely, they may have left their eggs or spun a cocoon in a protected niche. Woodpeckers haunt old trees. Look for holes that woodpeckers have chiseled in the bark as they hunted for insects.

SAP

The lifeblood of a tree is sap. It often oozes through small holes in the bark. Look carefully, you may find it hardened there in many artistic shapes.

LEAVES

Leaves use sunlight to manufacture food for the tree. The leaves of each kind of tree (maple, oak, beech, etc.) have distinctive shapes. Collect some leaves and compare their likenesses and differences. Some trees, such as the pine, have needles. Needles are leaves too.

FLOWERS

The fragile wild flowers that you may find, probably got their start in the springtime, before the leaves of the trees grew densely overhead, shutting out the sunlight. A flower is one of the ways in which a plant produces another plant. Flowers die, leaving behind the seeds of the next generation. You may find the seeds packed in brightly colored berries. The seeds are scattered by various means across the forest floor to bloom another time. But, don't pick wild flowers. Many woodland flowers are rare. The lovely flowers you carry away with you, will wilt within minutes. Let them go to seed, to insure their presence in the forest again.

NON-FLOWERING PLANTS

Non-flowering plants grow in abundant variety in the forest. Mushrooms, for instance, have many shapes and colors, but they have neither roots nor flowers. Tree mushrooms appear in many shapes and colors too. They get their nourishment from the tree itself, slowly eating away its heart. Eventually, tree mushrooms help to decay the tree and return it to the earth. A guide book, as well as some of the pictures in this book, will help you identify non-flowering plants, and some wild flowers. (See *For Further Reading on this page.*)

DECAY

Decay leads to new life. Fallen trees are not signs of an unhealthy forest. In falling, the old trees give new seedlings the room and the light needed to survive. The forest fertilizes itself. Dead leaves litter the forest floor and finally decay into it. Dead plants and animals add their own elements to enrich the earth and prepare it for new growth.

SOUNDS

The sounds in a forest can beckon you to adventure. If you stop, and quietly listen for a minute or two, the forest will surprise and reward you. A mysterious sound, filtering through leaves in the distance, can quicken your imagination. What is it? Could it be a deer traveling through the forest? A thrush foraging in the dead leaves? A flowing stream? Branches creaking in the wind? Try to track the sound to its source. You will find and see the forest in all its complex detail. It will widen your experience and sharpen your senses.

Read this story to your child or a young companion(s), then set out on an adventure together. You will join the multitude of people whose consciousness has been sharpened through discovering *The Floor of the Forest.*

FOR FURTHER READING

Shuttleworth, Floyd S., and Zim, Herbert S. Non-Flowering Plants, *Golden Press, N.Y. 1967.*

Smith, Alexander H., The Mushroom Hunter's Field Guide, *University of Michigan Press, Ann Arbor, Michigan, 1963.*

Wherry, Edgar T., The Fern Guide, *Doubleday & Co., Garden City, New York, 1961; also The Southern Fern Guide, 1964.*

Zim, Herbert S., and Martin, Alexander C., Trees, A Guide to Familiar American Trees, *Golden Press, New York, 1956.*

Audubon, *published by the National Audubon Society, 950 Third Avenue, New York.*